The Historical
Miles and Nina
(Civil Rights Movement)

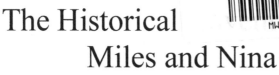

Volume I

Latasha L. Bethea

Illustrated by Keisha Otey Clay

Copyright © 2017 by Latasha L. Bethea, MACE, MSW, LCSW

The Historical Adventures of Miles and Nina (Civil Rights
Movement)
by Latasha L. Bethea, MACE, MSW, LCSW

Printed and Bound in the United States of America

ISBN-13: 978-1974585977
ISBN-10: 1974585972

Unless otherwise indicated, Scripture quotations used in this book
are from King James Version (KIV) of the Bible

www.createspace.com

Dedication

This book is dedicated to my grandmothers, stepfather, and beloved cousin

Lillie Mae Bethea
Susie Ella Daniels
John Wilbert Lindsey
Sherry Marie Lee

Forever in my heart!

Acknowledgements

First, I would like to thank God for His many blessings and the passion to write. He has allowed me to use writing, the very thing I have struggled with throughout life, as a platform to attest to His divine power. 2 Corinthians 12:9 says, "But He said to me, my grace is sufficient for you, for my strength is made prefect in weakness." Like Apostle Paul, I, too boast in my weaknesses, that God can use me in a humble state.

To my mother Doris R. Bethea, you have been my #1 cheerleader from the beginning of my life! You have been my wise counsel, supporter, and encourager through it all. I am grateful to have you as my mother! Love you much, Mama Love!

To my dad, John Wilbert Lindsey, you transitioned to be with the Lord before getting a chance to see all that God had in store for me. You always told me I was the Boss! Now I am trying to make boss moves! I hope you are proud of me! Love you forever!

To my father, Michael A. Sutton thank you for the prayers, words of wisdom, support, free labor, and tons of laughs! You always come through when I need you! I guess I got some of this creative writing from you! Love you much!

To my grandfather, James Carroll Sutton, thank you for the love, support, and the laughs!

To my aunts, Esther Clegg, Myrtle Ingram, Brenda Sutton Pemberton, and to my uncles, Connell Daniels, James Sutton, and Roger Bethea, thank you for the love, support, free labor, and encouragement!

To ALL of my cousins (too many to name one by one) thank you, thank you, thank you for all the support and encouragement in whatever event I do. You all are always in the crowd! Love you all to the moon and back!

To my sister-friends who are there when I need you. Wanda Lindsey Eaddy, Latasha Dean Chestnutt, Charnelle Green, Katina Braswell, Shameika Stokes, and Adrienne Williams. Thank you for listening to me whine and complain at times, but still encourage me to keep going. Thank you for the support, advice, correction, prayers, and free labor! I love and appreciate each of you!

To my spiritual mentors, Mother Ruth J. Mosley, Rev. Dr. Richelle B. White, and Pastor Rita McLean, thank you for the prayers, correction, advice, words of wisdom, and encouragement! You all keep me going even when I prefer to throw in the towel! Thank you for all that you do to help me with my spiritual growth! Your work is not in vain!

Special Thanks

To **Celestine Shepard Hinnant**, thank you for being the best editor! You always come through when I need you! I appreciate our friendship as well as your English skills!

To **Keisha Otey Clay,** thank you so much for your willingness to illustrate my first book! Your artistic abilities are truly a gift. I appreciate our friendship! I look forward to seeing where God is going to take you!

To **Lindse M. Owens,** thank you for your guidance in the publishing process! We both know I did not know which way to go! I wish you many blessings on your new journey!

To **Tamara Stanley,** thank you so much for converting Keisha Clay's illustrations into the digital graphics I needed in a short period of time! Thank you so much! I wish your company Red Palm Designs & Marketing much success in your future endeavors!

Endorsements

"The Historical Adventures of Miles and Nina" is lit! It is a page turner from beginning to end. Latasha Bethea presents a historically and culturally accurate snapshot of Black History in a way that is creative, relevant, hopeful and exciting. This book belongs in the hands of young people everywhere!

Rev. Richelle B. White, PhD
Professor of Youth Ministry
Kuyper College, Grand Rapids, MI

I feel like this book helps my generation see how we are so caught up in social media such as Snapchat and Instagram that we do not know enough about our history. *"The Historical Adventures of Miles and Nina"* shows us that if we would just research and explore our history, it would make a big difference in our lives. I enjoyed reading the book because it was informative and it made me want to know more about Black History, as well as my family's history. Most kids my age don't know what their grandparents or great-grandparents did to help make the Civil Rights Movement change the world.

Atirra McIver, 12

This new informational novel will change the minds of many, both young and old for many years to come. Ms. Latasha Bethea has written a funny, easy to read, yet serious, story that will teach the younger generation about our truthful past and yet remind the older generation of the past obstacles through the struggles for Civil Rights. This message is delivered through two relatable kids, whose time travel experience will open your heart and mind while inspiring you to share your own story.

Egypt Matthews, 16

"The Historical Adventures of Miles and Nina" offers a historical journey into African-American History that brings history to life through the lens of kids. This journey will move and inspire young readers to investigate history and make connections beyond social media to the struggles and triumphs of African-American people. Be engaged. Be inspired. Be affirmed. Knowledge is Power!

Ms. Charnelle E. Green
School Administrator
Guilford County Schools

Table of Contents

Prologue

Hi, my name is Sherry Sutton, African-American Studies professor at Chicago State University. I must admit being a wife, mother, and full-time professor can be a little difficult to juggle at times but my husband Nathan and I have worked hard to provide a safe, loving, and learning home environment for our children Nina and Miles. Nathan is an electrical engineer who works long hours to provide for our family. We are your typical hardworking family from the southside of Chicago in the Pullman area where Nathan and I grew up. We made a pact that once we got married, we would raise our family in our hometown. Pullman has changed over the years and not for the good, but we are determined to stay right here. Nathan and I both have a love for our African-

American culture especially when it comes to learning new information about Black History. We have worked very hard to make sure that our children are well-rounded individuals. It is our priority, every opportunity we get, to teach them about our family roots and Black History while exposing them to educational activities.

Our 13-year old daughter Nina is a beautiful, intelligent, and sometimes sassy young lady. She loves anything that has to do with fashion, art, and music. She is an honor roll student but her peers are starting to influence her way of thinking. Nina was once passionate about learning Black History. When she became a teen, her passion for learning Black History started to shift. She developed a mindset that if it happened prior to the development of social media, it is no longer relevant! She is starting to turn into a social media junkie, craving online attention.

Miles on the other hand, is a lot like his father and I with the passion for learning. He is an honor roll student and determined to be an engineer like his father one day. He is very focused, determined and inquisitive which is annoying to his sister at times. I am fearful that his passion for learning will start to decline due to the outside influences in our toxic society. Chicago does not have the best reputation in the news or on social media, but it is our home. Nathan and I are determined to give Nina and Miles everything they need and maybe a few of their wants in order to become successful individuals from Pullman Chicago.

Nina and Miles are my heart because I want the best for them. I am struggling to keep their desire for learning Black History ignited and growing. Somehow, I will have to figure out how to keep them both engaged and interested in learning Black History.

Oh, how I wish my Grandma Lillie was here! She always had clever ways to keep me interested in learning about our history. If she was here, she would know exactly what to do.

Chapter 1

The Family History

"Kids, come downstairs. I want to show you all something," yelled their mother from the family room. Nina and Miles made their way downstairs to see what their mother was so pressed to show them. In the middle of the family room was a large wooden trunk, and their mom was sitting on the floor in front of it.

"Mama, what's so important about this old dusty box?" Nina asked, while folding her arms with an attitude.

"It is not just an old dusty box, Nina, and unfold your arms unless I need to do it for you."

Nina dropped her arms, and her attitude before her mother helped her make an attitude adjustment.

"So, what is it Ma?" Miles asked as he ran his hand across the decorative carvings on the lid of the wooden box. "This is a cedar hope chest that belonged to my grandmother and your Great-Grandmother Lillie Mae Daniels."

"Wow, that's dope Ma," Miles replied.

"Miles, what did I tell you about using slang in this house?"

"My bad Ma. Oops, I apologize."

Nina was busy texting one of her friends instead of engaging in the conversation with her mother and Miles.

"Nina put that phone away!" her mother demanded in a stern voice.

Nina quickly slid her phone into the back pocket of her jeans before her mom could take it away for an extended period of time.

"Ok Ma. What is the purpose of the hope chest?" Miles asked.

"Good question, Miles. During Grandma Lillie's time, it was used to collect items, such as clothing, linens, and other family heirlooms in anticipation of a young woman's marriage."

"Ok, so basically a treasure chest?" Miles asked.

"Well, Miles I guess so. I never thought about it that way," she chuckled.

"Mama, thanks for the quick history lesson. May I go back upstairs now?" Nina interjected.

"Nina, my love, your Instagram and Twitter friends will be there when you get back upstairs. I am trying to pass on some family history to you and Miles," Mother stated in a calm but firm voice.

"Yeah, Nina, pay attention and learn something for a change!" Miles added.

"Miles, I don't need your input when I am talking to your sister!" Mother replied.

"Sorry. Ma, can we look inside?" Miles asked with excitement in his voice.

"Absolutely son," she responded with a smile on her face.

Miles quickly unlocked the latches on the front of the hope chest and pushed the lid up. There were several linens on top that his mother quickly removed in order to get to the family heirlooms. The first thing that caught Miles's attention

16

was an eyeglass case. He grabbed the case and opened it up. Inside was a pair of Grandma Lillie's eyeglasses.

"These are some funny looking glasses." Miles said in between chuckles.

"These glasses were called cat glasses because the frames are shaped like cat eyes," Mother explained.

"I think they are kinda cute, you know retro. I'm sure people will be rocking these again pretty soon," Nina interjected.

Nina put the glasses on and did a runway walk across the family room.

Miles fell onto the floor laughing until tears ran down his face, "Bruh, you got me weak."

"Shut up Miles, you don't know fashion with your four eyes," Nina retorted referring to Miles's glasses.

"Kids, you all stop playing and focus. Nina, you are correct! Alot of things come back in style," said their mother.

"Yeah like Miles's haircut," Nina blurted out in between laughs.

"Yo, my hair cut is one of a kind. Nina, you're bugging!" Miles said with confidence.

"Technically, Miles, Nina is right, that style was popular back in my youthful day. During the time of Pumas, gold earrings and chains, house parties, and Kid and Play," stated their mother with a smile on her face as she briefly reminisced her childhood.

"Kid and who?" Miles asked.

"Never mind," sighed their mother while shaking her head. "Let's see what else is in here."

"Aww, look. Here is a picture of Grandma Lillie in front of the Woolworth Store in Greensboro, North Carolina. It looks like she is sporting her stylish cat glasses in the picture."

"May I see it Mama?" Nina asked.

Her mother immediately handed her the picture, and Nina intensely looked at the photo of her great-grandmother. This was the first time she had seen an actual picture of her great-grandmother even though her mother talked about her all the time.

"Wow Grandma Lillie was a beautiful woman!" Nina stated. "She has dimples just like you and me, Mama!"

"Yes, we got our dimples as well as our hazel eyes from her too, even though you can't tell it from the black and white photo. My grandmother was a kind and an intelligent lady. She was hard working, firm, but also lots of fun. Oh, how I miss my grandmother. I remember spending a lot of time with her during the summer back in Sanford, North Carolina. My grandmother was a master chef in the kitchen. She loved to cook big meals each time my parents and I would come down to visit. Her cornbread fritters with collards and fried chicken was one of my favorite meals."

"Man, that sounds delicious!" Miles licked his lips.

"My grandmother was the best! I really wish you two would have had the opportunity to really get to know her before she transitioned to be with the Lord."

Mother quickly wiped away a tear that slid down her face before the kids noticed she was crying.

"It looks like Grandma Lillie was coming from school based on this picture. She has school books in her arms," Miles said while leaning over Nina's shoulder to look at the picture.

"Good observation, Miles. That is a strong possibility. Grandma Lillie attended W.B. Wicker School down in Sanford, and after she graduated, she was accepted to North Carolina A&T University in Greensboro. So, this picture was probably taken while she was a student at A&T."

"Ok, cool, so Grandma Lillie was an Aggie like dad!" Miles responded as he shouted Aggie Pride throughout the room.

"Yes, Miles, but don't get too hyped about them Aggies!" warned his mother as she shouted Bronco Pride to represent her alma mater Fayetteville State University.

They started giggling over the college battle about which of these two historically black universities was the best which is always a debate in their home.

"Ma, so who is the lady in the picture with Grandma Lillie?" Miles directed their attention back to the items from the hope chest.

"Oh, this is one of Grandma Lillie's childhood best friends, Mrs. Emma Sue Richardson. They were close like sisters, so close that we called her Aunt Cat. She and Grandma Lillie were inseparable! They went through school and even to college together."

"So, they were tight like Tasha and me," Nina replied as she mentioned her best friend.

"Yes, they were very close. After they graduated from college they both ended up getting married to their college sweethearts and moving to separate states to start their families and careers. They always stayed in contact with each other. I think Aunt Cat moved to Mississippi or Alabama with her family. After Grandma Lillie died, we lost contact with Aunt Cat. I used to love watching her and my grandma laugh and share stories like they were schoolgirls again when Aunt Cat would visit for a few weeks every summer."

"Wow, I wonder how Aunt Cat is doing?" stated their mother. "Maybe I can locate one of her daughters on Facebook. Ok, let's see what other good stuff is down in here."

Nina reached into the hope chest and pulled out several beads of various color. "Mama why would Grandma Lillie have Mardi Gras beads? I thought you said she lived in North Carolina."

"Yes, she lived in North Carolina, but she also had family on her mother's side in New Orleans. I remember her telling me stories of her visiting family during the summer in the Bayou. I'm sure she probably participated in a few Mardi Gras parades back in her day." Mother replied.

"So, we have family in North Carolina and New Orleans?" Miles asked.

"Yes, we do Miles, but unfortunately, we have not been able to attend some of the family reunions due to your father's and my busy work schedule. But, hopefully, you will get a chance to meet some of your cousins from down south pretty soon."

"I will pass on that trip Ma," said Nina, "I heard it is real humid down there! I can't be sweating out my blowout nor do I plan to eat alligator and stuff all day."

"Nina, you are a mess baby girl," her mother chuckled. "What do you know about eating alligator?"

"I watch that show Swamp People sometimes when I am bored. So, I know enough about Louisiana, I am good right here in Chi-city."

"Nina, there is more to Louisiana than what you see on TV. New Orleans is filled with excitement, delicious cuisines, and a rich history. You are going to get enough of believing everything you see on television," their mother warned them.

"Grandma Lillie also used to visit Montgomery, Alabama as a child. I believe that is where some of Grandma Lillie's father's family was from. During that time, the Jim Crow laws were used to keep black and white people separated. It was some very harsh times for African Americans in the deep south."

"Ma, what were some of the Jim Crow laws?" Miles asked.

"Miles, you know the rule in this house!"

"Yes, Ma, if I don't know it, research it!" Miles replied

"Well, it appears you and Nina have some research to do!" their mother replied.

"But Mama I did not ask about Jim Crow laws. Why do I have to do research?" Nina asked in protest.

"Well, first because I said so; second, it will give you a chance to learn more about the Civil Rights Movement and your Great-Grandma Lillie's life," Mother said.

"Dang, Miles, you and your 10,000 questions. Now we are both stuck doing research over the weekend," Nina replied with extreme attitude.

"Nina, stop being mean to your brother. I do expect you both to give a detailed report on Sunday during our family dinner. Your father and I will look forward to hearing what you have learned! Here, take the picture, beads, and eye glasses and see what you can find out about this era in Black History. I look forward to hearing your individual reports!" replied their mother with great emphasis on the word individual. Miles and Nina grabbed the objects and took off running upstairs to get started on their assignment.

Chapter 2

The Research

(Nina)

"Great job, Knucklehead! Now I am stuck doing unnecessary work over the weekend."

"Don't trip, Nina, I gotcha. Since I am the smart one in this duo. I'll have two outstanding reports ready for Sunday dinner before breakfast!" Miles replied.

"You are such a geek!" I said while rolling my eyes.

"Nina don't hate because I enjoy learning and everything I do is fire! You could be like me if you stopped spending all of your time on Snapchat, Instagram, and Twitter. I mean, seriously how many must you post of yourself in 24 hours? You have not changed that much in a day. How about you chill and take a selfie or something while I handle this?" Miles replied.

Whew, I was glad Miles was willing to do both reports, but I could not show it. I stretched out on the bean bag chair in Miles's room while he searched the internet for information about Jim Crow laws. I started to browse through videos on YouTube when I saw a light flicker out the corner of my eye. I looked up but did not see what could have caused the light. So, I went back to browsing videos. After an hour had passed,

24

Mama yelled from downstairs to ask how the research was going.

Miles yelled, "It's coming along great, Ma!"

"Nina, are you helping your brother?" replied Mama.

"Yes Ma. We are getting it done," I said convincingly.

"Nina, don't be lying to me! I will know if Miles ended up doing both reports!" Mother replied.

Mama always had a way of recognizing when we were lying even when we put on our best academy award-winning performance.

"We are good Mama, I promise," I yelled back. "Miles, hurry and give me a book on Civil Rights in case Mama comes up stairs. I can at least at look like I am reading."

"You reading? Yeah right, Mama is not going to believe that," chuckled Miles.

"Whatever, Bruh!" I said and smacked my lips. I quickly grabbed a book off Miles's bookshelf and pretended to be reading. I never heard mama come up the stairs, so I tossed the book on his bed and went back to my movie.

An hour and a half had passed by, and Miles was in his "geek zone" when a flash of light caught my eye again. It was coming from Grandma Lillie's glasses. "Ok, clearly, I must need a break from my phone because my eyes are playing tricks on me," I said to myself. But before I could finish my thought, the eye glasses lit up again, and this time the frame changed colors.

"Miles, stop playing!" I yelled.

Miles turned around and looked at me like I was tripping.

"Nina what are you talking about, Bruh? I have been looking at this computer for almost two hours. Nobody got time to be playing," Miles replied.

"So how did you turn Grandma Lillie's eye glass frames red? Look!" I pointed to the glasses.

Miles turned around and sure enough Grandma Lillie's glasses were now red, which is no where close to the black frames we pulled out of the hope chest earlier.

"Man, that is hot but I didn't do it. Let me check them out!" Miles exclaimed as he reached for the glasses.

"Boy, don't touch those glasses. Something crazy might happen," I yelled.

"Like what Nina?" Miles interjected.

Before I responded, my curious yet impulsive little brother grabbed the glasses.

"See, Chicken Little. Nothing happened!" Miles stated in his cocky "I know it all" voice.

Just as he was spinning the glasses in his hands, they began to vibrate, and there was a bright flash that blinded us for a second. I was able to grab hold of Miles's arm before everything started spinning. I don't know what happened but when I was finally able to open my eyes, I realized quickly we were no longer on the southside of Chicago. Where, I didn't know, but we were definitely not in Chicago!

Chapter 3

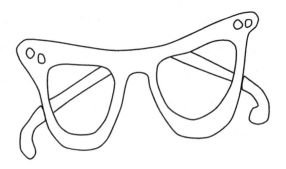

The Transport

(Miles)

"What in the world happened, Nina?" I grabbed my head to focus because I was feeling dizzy.

Nina looked like she had seen a ghost, and her pecan brown face was pale as if all the blood had left it. Before I could snap Nina out of her trance, I was hit with unbearable heat. My armpits started sweating like I just ran the 400 in the Olympics. "Nina, Nina, snap out of it! Where are we?"

Nina snapped out of it really quick because her smart mouth went from zero to one hundred in a matter of seconds. "See what you did, Miles!" Nina yelled. "You are always doing something, and I am left to get us out of the mess every time. I told your bubblehead not to touch the glasses, but nope, you did it anyway. Now look, we are in the middle of I don't know where and it's hot like fire!"

"Are you done, Sis?" I asked.

"No, I am not done!" Nina said, but she chilled out once she noticed that people were starting to stare at us. She took a deep breath and tried to calm down, but she still smacked me in the back of my head.

Nina was tripping so hard that I did not realize we were dressed differently until I looked at my feet and saw that my fresh to death J's were replaced with some leather black church shoes. Now I was starting to get hyped up at this devastating discovery.

"Are you done?" Nina asked in a sarcastic voice.

"Man, mom is going to kill me if I don't get my J's back." I screamed as I paced back and forth.

"Bruh, it is not that serious. I am sure there is an explanation for all of this. When I get us out of this mess, I bet the next time you will listen to me," Nina replied.

"Man, this heat is crazy. I need some water." I started looking around for a water fountain.

We quickly spotted a water fountain over by what appeared to be the town's grocery store. We ran across the street towards the fountain. Just as I was about to take a take a sip to quench my thirst, a little old lady carrying a bag of groceries, pulled me by the arm from the fountain.

Before I could ask why she was tripping, she said "Chile, don't you see that fountain is for white folks? We Negroes have to drink from that colored fountain over there."

Nina and I looked at each other with a puzzled look when she said, "colored fountain."

The little old lady pointed up to a sign with big black letters that read "Whites Only." Immediately, Nina and I both realized that we were a long way from home and somehow traveled back in time. This would explain our crazy attire and these segregated activities happening right before our eyes.

"Y'all youngins must be from up North? Y'all need to get use to these Jim Crow laws before you get yourselves in some unwanted trouble down here in Montgomery, Alabama!" said the old lady.

"Ma'am, what is today's date?" Nina asked.

"Honey, it is March 5, 1955. I tell you, it is an unusually hot day for it to be winter. But weather in Montgomery is tricky in March, hot during the day, bone-chilling cold at night," chuckled the little lady.

"Nina," I tried to whisper, "Jim Crow laws is what Ma was trying to get us to research. Now it is starting to make sense. I guess grandma's glasses somehow transported us back into time prior to integration and into the era of segregation under the Jim Crow laws."

The little old lady was looking at me like I had lost my mind. Nina elbowed me in my side to make me shut-up.

"Ma'am, please don't pay my little brother any attention. He has such a wild imagination," Nina stated. "Do you mind directing us to the nearest bus stop?"

"I sure can, honey, matter of fact I am heading that way myself. Follow me," replied the little old lady.

Nina and I followed the little lady up a few blocks, then across the street to the nearest bus stop in Downtown Montgomery.

Chapter 4

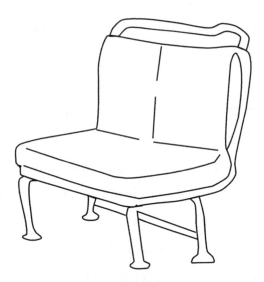

The Refusal

(Nina)

While Miles and I sat with the little lady waiting for the bus, my mind was on turbo speed trying to figure out how to find our way back home. The only thing we had was a bag with a few of Grandma Lillie's things and a few dollars. While I was trying not to freak out, Miles was doing what he does best asking a million questions! I jumped into the conversation to get some questions answered before the bus arrived.

"Ma'am, may I ask you a question?"

"Sure, honey, and by the way you can call me Mrs. Emma.

"Nice to meet you Mrs. Emma. My name is Nina, and this is my little brother Miles," I replied.

"You mean intelligent brother," Miles interjected, which caused Mrs. Emma to chuckle.

"Whatever Bruh. Mrs. Emma can you tell us more about these Jim Crow laws?"

"Chile, there is not enough time in the day to tell you about these ridiculous laws! I think some of these foolish white folks add new ones to the list daily. Jim Crow laws are used to keep us Negros from having the same rights and freedoms as white folks. But let me tell you a few that will at least keep you out of trouble while you two are visiting. First off you cannot eat at the same lunch counters, drink from the same fountains, or use the same bathrooms as white people. Always look for the "colored" signs. I am going to tell you right now, our fountains, bathrooms, and eating areas are not kept up or clean as the white folks. So, what we Negroes have learned to do is not eat nothing before coming to town and pack our own snacks if were going to be there for a while. So, you don't have the need to use those down right nasty facilities. There is even a law to keep us from buying vanilla ice cream except on the Fourth of July."

Miles jumped up, "No vanilla ice cream, that is crazy! Nina, you know vanilla is my favorite!"

Mrs. Emma leaned over and whispered, "It is my favorite too, Miles, but it is not allowed." She continued to go over rule after rule until I was experiencing information overload. I guess she noticed that I was looking a little overwhelmed.

Mrs. Emma stopped and said, "Nina honey, are you alright?"

I faintly said, "Yes ma'am, but it is a lot to take in all at once."

Miles butted in "Yes, it is way too much, Mrs. Emma. You see where we are from we can sit and eat where we want. We dress in comfortable clothes while loosing up his necktie. We go to school with people from all ethnic backgrounds Asian, White, Latino, you name it."

"Is that so," Mrs. Emma replied. "Now where are you children from again?"

"Miles, chill out with all those stories," I shot him a serious look. "Mrs. Emma, we are visiting from Chicago."

"Nina, I'm starting to see what you mean, Miles definitely has an imagination," chuckled Mrs. Emma.

Before Miles could start to protest, the Capital Height's bus approached our stop. There were a number of people both black and white on the bus. I did notice that all the black people were at the rear of the bus.

Mrs. Emma stopped us before the bus door opened. "I forgot to tell y'all that black folks sit at the back of the bus in the colored section. If the bus gets crowded, we have to give up our seat to any white person that needs a seat."

"Why?" Miles asked.

"Because is it the law, and if you don't, they will haul your hind parts to jail," Mrs. Emma said. "Now when we get on here, make sure y'all sit with me."

The thought of going to jail was terrifying to Miles and me. Once we paid our fare we immediately followed Mrs. Emma to the back of the bus.

The Capital Heights bus made a couple of more stops in the downtown area. It was obvious that people were getting off work and students were getting on heading home from school. I noticed that a young black girl a little bit older than me, I guess around 15-years-old, got on the bus carrying her school books. She sat in the row in front of us. The bus ride was fairly quiet for it to be packed with people both white and black. The next stop a white lady got on the bus. I noticed that the white lady was standing in the white sections looking for a seat, but there was none. Suddenly, the driver looked in the mirror above his seat and yelled for the young girl and three other black women on her row to move to the back. Immediately, the three women moved. In the midst of them moving, a pregnant black woman got on the bus. The pregnant lady had no idea what was going on, so she sat right beside the young girl. I immediately felt something was about to go down since, Mrs. Emma already told us that Negros were forced to give up their seats for white people. So, the rude bus driver told the pregnant lady and the young girl to move. The pregnant lady said she was not getting up, she had paid her fare, and she did not feel like standing. Then the young girl said, "I am not going to get up either." Now you could feel the tension on the bus, just as thick as of the humid air we were breathing in. The bus driver stopped the bus and threatened to call the police, but both women sat firmly in their seats.

When police got on the bus, a black man sitting across from us got up to let the pregnant lady have his seat. I guess he did not want to see the police cause any harm to her or her unborn baby. But the young girl still refused to move! I was

36

proud yet scared at the same time for her. The police grabbed her and forcibly removed her from the bus and arrested her. My heart was racing, and I could not get the girl's face out of my mind. I was quiet the rest of the ride wondering what happened to the young girl who stood up to the police and these dumb Jim Crow laws.

Chapter 5

The Discovery

(Nina)

Finally, the bus made it to Mrs. Emma's stop. We sat there as she gathered her things. I guess she came to the realization that we were lost because all of a sudden, she turned around and said, "Y'all sitting here looking long-eyed, help this old lady with her stuff." We gladly jumped, gathered her things off the bus, and walked Mrs. Emma to her home.

As we were getting close to a little house with a white picket fence, Mrs. Emma started to slow down so I assumed this was her house. The yard was nice and neat with little indications that spring was slowly approaching. Mrs. Emma invited us into her home to have a little bite to eat which was right on time since Miles and I both were starving.

"Y'all children, follow me into the kitchen to wash your hands in the water basin."

"What is a water basin, Mrs. Emma?" Miles asked.

She pointed to a stand in the corner of her kitchen. The top held a deep, yet, wide porcelain bowl and at the bottom of the stand was a large pitcher with the same design as the bowl full of water.

Mrs. Emma said "Take that lye soap and pour the water over your hands to clean them, while I put these groceries away. After I get cleaned up, I will fix us all a little lunch. I know you children are probably starving by now."

"Thank you, Mrs. Emma. Miles and I really do appreciate your hospitality."

"Anytime honey, go make yourselves comfortable in the living room while I put these sandwiches together."

"Mrs. Emma, may I stay in here and ask you a few more questions about the Jim Crow laws?" Miles asked.

"You sure can!" replied Mrs. Emma.

While Miles was busy asking Mrs. Emma a million questions, I looked at some of the family portraits she had hanging all over her walls. You could tell by the pictures that she had a large family. While I was looking at pictures, I ran across a picture that looked very familiar. After I examined the picture, it hit me! This is the same picture mama had in the hope chest of Great-Grandma Lillie and her friend Aunt Cat. Why would Mrs. Emma have a picture of Grandma Lillie and her best friend? I was so far in my thoughts, that I did not realize Mrs. Emma had come into the living room. She had a tray filled with mini sandwiches, large cookies, and lemonade.

"I see you found the picture of my best friend Lillie and me in front of Woolworth's Five and Dime Store in Greensboro. You see, that was our senior year in college. I tell you we had some good ole' times back then. Yes, Lillie and I were some sassy ladies back then with our cat glasses. We were so stylish that people used to call me Cat instead of Emma."

Miles looked at me as if the light bulb just came on in his head, "Nina, this is Aunt Cat. Mama was telling us about her this morning," he said with excitement in his voice.

Mrs. Emma had a surprised look on her face, "How did you know people called me Aunt Cat?"

"Oh, that was a lucky guess," I said, "by the pictures on the wall you have to be someone's aunt, right? Miles, how about we do less talking and more eating?"

Just as Miles was reaching for a sandwich, Mrs. Emma caught his hand. "No sir, we say grace around here before eating anything. What are they teaching you all in the North?" Miles quickly apologized and bowed his head for the blessing of the food.

After we feasted on the delicious sandwiches Mrs. Emma prepared, we were both ready to dive into her plate of homemade cookies. "Go ahead and get you a few of those tea cookies while I go to my room to make a call," Mrs. Emma said as she walked down the hall towards a room in the back of the house.

I knew Mrs. Emma's mind was spinning trying to figure out who we were and why my big mouth brother knew her nickname was Cat. "Miles, hand me the bag with Grandma Lillie's things in it. We have to get out of here before Mrs. Emma comes back," I said with urgency in my voice.

"Why?" Miles asked between bites of his cookie.

"Because we have to find our way back home. We can't stay here in 1955, duh!" I reached into the bag and pulled out the identical picture Mrs. Emma had on her coffee table of her and Grandma Lillie. I stood up and demanded Miles to do the same even though he was too busy trying to stuff cookies in his pockets. "Dude put them cookies down, we got to get out of here!" Miles rolled his eyes, but for the first time on this journey, he followed my instructions. We both held on to the picture and closed our eyes, but nothing happened. We were still in Mrs. Emma's house looking crazy.

"Miles, why are we still here? Nothing is happening like with Grandma Lillie's glasses." I was about to start tripping, but Miles stopped me.

"Bruh, chill so I can think," Miles replied. After what seemed like forever, he snapped his fingers. "I got it! Remember when we were at home, I was spinning grandma's glasses in my hand. Maybe if we spin the picture, it will trigger the portal to open up."

"Miles, hurry up and do it. I think I hear Mrs. Emma coming up the hall," I whispered. Miles placed the picture on the coffee table to spin it. I held his hand and just as he predicted, the picture started shooting flashes of various colors. Then all of a sudden, we were whisked away, hopefully back to Miles's room!

Chapter 6

The Sit-in

(Miles)

Even after my stomach settled from that second rollercoaster ride, I was too afraid to open my eyes. My heart raced with the anticipation of being back in my room, in my chill clothes, and in my freshly purchased J's.

"Miles, open your eyes, boy!" yelled Nina

"I will open my eyes only if we are back in Chicago."

"Well, I guess you will be standing out here with your eyes closed like a clown," Nina replied.

"Dang, I thought we were traveling back home. Bruh, I am tired of walking around in these tight spit-shined dress shoes and slacks."

"Well, at least you are not stuck wearing a Sunday dress and white ankle shoes," Nina said.

After looking Nina up and down, I busted out laughing. "You do look like you are about to recite an Easter speech," I blurted out in between my chuckles.

"Well, at least I don't look like a mini version of SpongeBob," Nina replied.

"Whatever, Nina. So where are we now?"

"How am I supposed to know Miles? We got here at the same time, clown." Nina rolls her eyes.

"One day, your eyes are going to get stuck like that Nina."

"Boy, please, that is an old wives' tale," Nina said as she smacked me in the back of the head. "Look, Miles, there is the Woolworth building that was in the picture with Grandma Lillie and Mrs. Emma."

Nina and I crossed over South Elm Street to get a closer look at the building. It appeared to be a busy store with people entering and exiting with shopping bags.

Nina and I stepped into the store and noticed that it was filled with all types of things, such as clothing, shoes, furniture, houseware and much more. It reminded me of an old-school Walmart with everything you need for your home. The two biggest things that separated Woolworth's from Walmart were the prices and the lunch counter.

"Nina look, this stuff is dirt cheap! This bag of candy is only five cents! I have clearly died and gone to heaven," I proclaimed.

"Miles, put that candy down! We are not here to shop but figure out why Grandma Lillie's picture brought us here."

Man, my sister can be a stick in the mud at times. While I was placing the candy back where I got it from, I noticed four black men walking towards the store. They looked older than high school students, but not by much. They wore long trench coats, and one of the guys was very tall and had on an army uniform. The men came in and walked to the side of the store that black people were allowed. I saw that they purchased toothpaste and stuff. They did nothing out of the norm, so I went on my way looking around with Nina, but I kept glancing back at the men. All of a sudden, the four guys started heading towards the front of the store, but instead of heading out the door, they went over to the lunch counter. I watched as they sat down beside some white people who were there eating. Earlier, I had already peeped out the signs for whites only at the lunch counter. I got an eerie feeling that these guys were about to get into some serious trouble. By the look of the faces of the white people that were at the counter, I was sure it was about to get lit.

"Nina, look. Those men just sat down at the lunch counter," I whispered.

"So, what's the big deal, Miles? I guess they are hungry like everyone else."

"No, it is more than that, Nina. Look at the sign," I replied.

"Uh-oh, Miles. Let's get closer and see how this is going to play out," said Nina.

We found a hiding spot in between a rack of clothes to get a better view of what was going on as well as to try to hear the conversation. One of the men politely asked the white waitress for a cup of coffee. The waitress quickly refused and reminded them that colored folks were not allowed at the counter. I noticed that the men had an unusual calmness about the situation, as if they were on a mission. The waitress hurried off to get the store manager. I could tell by his cherry red face that he was not happy when he approached the four Negro men sitting at his white-only counter. He demanded that they leave but the men sat there. It reminded me of the young girl on the bus Nina and I saw earlier that day with Mrs. Emma. They had indescribable boldness to stand up for their rights even in the midst of extreme danger. The white customers were getting very impatient and starting to leave because the men were there.

"Nina, it looks like Woolworth will be losing some money today," I chuckled.

"Good, it appears the only way to get people in authority to listen to you, is to hit them where it hurts the most, in their pockets."

"True indeed Sis, true indeed. Well it looks like it is going to be a long night for them. Let's get out of here." I walked proudly out of the Woolworth store because I had a feeling the four men just took a bold step towards equal rights for everyone.

"Nina, I think we are not going to make it home until we visit all the places Grandma Lillie went based on the three items from the bag."

"I have come to that same conclusion Miles. Well, we are down to one item, so we might as well see where it is going to take us," said Nina.

"Yeah, you are right Nina. Hopefully we have not spent our whole weekend on this journey, because I don't want to hear your mouth, if we did!"

"It's cool, Miles, I am actually learning a lot," Nina replied.

"Aww man. Nina, get out the sun, I think you have lost your mind," I said as I pushed her under a shady area outside the Woolworth store.

"Boy, stop pushing me before I crack your blockhead!" Nina yelled.

"Oh, yeah, you are back. I thought I lost you for a minute," I chuckled.

I reached into our bag and found Grandma Lillie's last item, the colorful Mardi Gras beads. "Alright, Sis let's bounce." Nina and I joined hands while I started spinning the beads around my index finger. I guess Nina and I had gotten used to the ride now because it only felt like seconds to get to our last destination.

Chapter 7

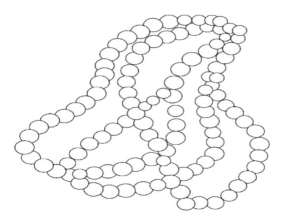

The Integration

(Nina)

I had already mentally braced myself for the New Orleans humidity. By the time, we came to our stop in NOLA, my blowout had turned back to my natural curly hair state.

"Dang Nina, look at your hair," Miles busted out laughing.

"Shut up Miles. You are paying for my next trip to the Dominican shop for my blow out, bet."

"Bruh, you're tripping!" Miles replied.

"Tripping, hmmm, did you forget that you got us out here in this mess?" I yelled.

"Here we go again. What happened to you saying that it was cool and you are learning a lot?" Miles replied.

"Well, that thought went out the door when my hair turned into the Power Puff girls," I replied.

Miles busted out laughing again, but this time, I started laughing too. After I got a good look at my hair through one of the windows of one of the hundreds of cars parked down this street.

After we stopped giggling, we realized that people were gathering in front of some school off in the distance. "Miles, it looks like something big is happening over there. Maybe we are about to witness one of those Mardi Gras parades. Let's go check it out," I said.

When Miles and I got close enough, I saw that the school was William Frantz Elementary School. The name of the school looked familiar, but I could not recall why. The closer we got to the crowd the more we realized this was not a happy occasion and definitely not a gathering for a parade. There was a large gathering of angry white people of all ages and genders shouting racial slurs. I immediately grabbed Miles so we could hide before the angry mob spotted us in the crowd. We hid in the thicket around a wooded area near the school. The angry mob had protest signs, bats, car jacks, and other objects in their hands, like they were ready to go do some serious damage to someone or something.

"Wow, Nina, I wonder what got them so hyped up right now," Miles asked.

"Yeah, me too! But whatever it is, it does not look good," I said with my hands trembling on his shoulder. "Make sure we stay out of sight Little Bro," I said and pushed Miles's head farther down into the bushes. I really do love my brother even through I beat him up from time to time. While I was still lost in my train of thought, I spotted what the white people was upset about. All of a sudden, a cute little black girl in a little dress, ankle socks, dress shoes, and a ribbon hair bow on her head emerged from the crowd with white men with black suits and patches on their arm guarding her. The crowd did not intimidate her even though they were shouting hateful things to her. It was a clear indication that the men around her had to be the FBI or some form of law enforcement. When Miles saw her, he immediately recognized her.

"Nina, that is Ruby Bridges," Miles said.

"Ruby who?" I replied.

"Ruby Bridges. Remember Mama telling us about the seminar she went to on the effects of racism on children of the

51

1950s and 60s at Fayetteville State University last year? Mrs. Ruby Bridges Hall was one of the keynote speakers."

"Oh yeah, I forgot about that, she was the one that first integrated a school here in Louisiana.

"Well, that little girl is the woman Mama was talking about," Miles replied.

"Wow Miles, look how little she is, she can't be no more than 5-years-old. I can't believe these grown adults tripping over a child," I said with a deep sigh.

"I know what you mean Sis. This is just ludicrous! It looks like they are taking her into the school. Let's go check it out," said Miles.

Miles and I took off running fast, but as quiet as we could, to get inside of the school building without being seen by the angry crowd. We found an unlocked door on the backside of the school. We quietly ran down the hall of the school to look for Ruby. It took a while to locate her because she was not in a classroom but actually in the principal's office with a white lady. It appeared that this lady was Ruby's teacher. She was teaching a lesson as if there were a dozen kids in the office instead of just her and Ruby. I cannot imagine what was going on in her little head; she had to know that all this chaos was over her being in this all white school. I must admit, Ruby did not let the crowd or the things that were happening outside scare her. She looked calm, and she was very attentive to her teacher.

"Bruh, Ruby really is the real MVP! Look, she is not letting the ignorance of those foolish people keep her from her education. I am not sure that I would have been that brave."

"Me either, Nina, for real for real," Miles said with a concerned look on his face.

"What is wrong, Miles?" I asked while we were heading out the back door of William Frantz Elementary School.

"I am just thinking about the time frame. Nina, do you realize that some of our friends' grandparents could be some of those angry people back there making Ruby's life miserable? This event took place not too long ago and the more I think about the injustices of our people now, it looks like history is repeating itself. Bruh, it really is scary."

"I know what you mean Miles, but I don't think this journey was meant to make us fearful but to acknowledge the strength of our people to overcome even in the midst of extreme adversity. I mean, think about all the people we saw. They were young, but they made a major impact on society. So, we should be proud and know that we have the ability to make positive changes in our very own community," I said as we were walking.

Chapter 8

The Purpose

(Nina)

All of a sudden Miles and I heard a female voice say, "Mission accomplished." We both stopped dead in our tracks when we heard the voice, because there was no one around us. Then there was a bright light. It was so bright that it was hard to explain; it was almost as if it was a glimpse into the Heavens.

Miles and I covered our eyes from the brightness, but we could see an older lady coming towards us. She looked familiar the moment our eyes adjusted after the bright light went away. She was a short little lady with a slender frame. She was wearing her Sunday's best, but it was in all white.

"Lawd, lookatcha Nina and Miles! You babies are so adorable."

"Ma'am how do you know our names?" I asked.

"Why would I not know the names of my great-grandchildren? Now stop with all the questions and come and give your Grandma Lillie a hug."

We were both excited and shocked to see our great-grandmother right before our eyes. You see I was 3-years-old when Grandma Lillie passed away, and Miles was only a few months old. All we had were the pictures of her in her young years to go by. When I walked over to her and looked at her, I immediately remembered her hazel eyes and deep dimples when she smiled at me. I wrapped my arms around my great-grandmother and hugged her just has hard as she was hugging me. Miles then jumped in on the hug fest. After we separated from our embrace, you know Miles was ready to run his lips asking questions.

"Grandma Lillie, so you had something to do with us coming back in time?" Miles asked.

"I sure did. Miles, I have been watching y'all youngins, not just you two but the rest of my great-grands and your friends. And honestly baby, I did not like what I saw," said Grandma Lillie with a concerned look on her face. "You see, my loves, the stuff they are teaching you all in school is not the whole truth. It has been a lot of "whitewashing" going on of our history and making you children think that our history was not that bad or it was so long ago. Now you all walking around like Black History is boring and not important now, especially you, Nina."

"Yeah, Nina shame on you!" Miles interjected.

"Miles, sit your little self down before I jack a knot in your tail. I don't need your input either, while I am talking to your sister," Grandma Lillie said in a firm voice.

"Sorry, Grandma Lillie," Miles said while sitting on the bench next to her.

"Look here, my loves, you all come from greatness and it is critical that you all recognize this fact! The word of God tells us in Hosea that we are destroyed for lack of knowledge, because we rejected knowledge."

"What does that mean Grandma?" I asked.

"It means, for your generation, that you are being mentally destroyed by this garbage this society is feeding to you all though those social outlets y'all spend all that time on, that youbook and snapper and stuff."

"Hmmm, Grandma Lillie do you mean Facebook, Youtube and Snapchat?" I asked while chuckling.

"Well you know what I was talking about," chuckled Grandma Lillie. "Oh, and don't get me started on that music you all be listening to, especially that ole song talking about Molly and Percocet. It is just a shame, and you all bopping around like it's an amazing song."

"Grandma Lillie, it is just music. The beat is fire!" Miles interjected.

"See, that is where you are wrong honey. Music is one of the most powerful ways to plant thoughts in your mind. You listen to positive music, and you think positive things. But when you fill your mind with negative things, eventually it will overtake you. This is the ultimate plan used to keep us divided and oppressed. I am not talking about what I heard, this is what I know. But I know you babies do it to be cool or down with your homies."

"Homies?" Nina and Miles said in unison while giggling.

"Well your friends. Is that better?" Grandma Lillie asked.

"Yes, much better, Grandma Lillie. Please leave the slang to Miles and me," I said

"Ok deal. Look sweethearts, it is time for me to get back to the heavenly realm, but I have a few more nuggets of wisdom for you. Remember, if you do not learn from your mistakes, you are more than likely going to experience them again until you learn. This is what is happening in history right now. It is repeating itself. During my time, young black men were being lynched in trees but now bullets from guns are the new ropes and the murderers are both black and white. It is impossible to gain respect when you don't know your own history, and I am not talking about that watered-down mess in your school history books either. This black on black crime has to stop with us before any other race of people start to acknowledge who we are as a people. Second, listen and respect your parents. It may seem at times that what they are telling you is restricting you from having fun, but remember they are parents, not your friends. Their job is to protect you, provide for you, and push you to be the best Miles and Nina you can be. So, don't let me see you all sassing your mother or father. They are all you got, and one day you will not have them. So, love them and respect them as long as you can. Last but not least, share with others what you have learned from this experience. It is critical! You youngins hear me?"

"Yes ma'am," Miles and I said in unison.

All of a sudden that bright light started to shine in the distant.

"Well Babies that's my cue. Now come over here and give your great-grandma some sugar."

Miles and I both embraced our great-grandmother one last time after giving her a kiss on her cheek.

As Grandma Lillie walked toward the light, Miles said, "There is no way Ma is going to believe that we met Grandma Lillie, Nina?"

"You are right Bruh," Nina replied.

Grandma Lillie turned around and said, "Y'all tell Moochie that I love her, and I'm very proud of the woman she has become!"

"Grandma Lillie who is Moochie?" I asked.

"It's your mother baby," she replied as she faded into the bright light.

Chapter 9

The Reveal

"Miles, Nina, wake up," said their mother. She shook both of them on the shoulder.

"Where are we?" Miles said in a sluggish voice.

"What do you mean, where are you? You and your sister up here sleeping instead of doing research! Look at you, Miss Sleeping Beauty," her mother replied as Nina struggled to wipe her eyes.

When Miles and Nina recognized their mother's voice they both jumped up and hugged her as if they had not seen her in years.

"Mama you don't know how glad we are to see you again!"

"Yes, Ma. That trip was unbelievable, but we are so glad to be back with you in Chicago!" Miles stated with excitement.

"Huh? Trip, What trip? Back in Chicago. Wow, you two were dreaming hard!" their mother replied with a chuckle.

"No Ma, it's true. We went through this portal back into the Civil Rights Movement. We saw the guys from Greensboro who did a sit-in at the Woolworth Store," Miles explained.

"Yeah Mama, and we saw the 15-year old girl who refused to give up her seat on a segregated bus in Montgomery, Alabama, and Ruby Bridges in New Orleans!" Nina interjected.

"Wait, wait, wait, so you mean to tell me you saw Ezell Blair Jr., Franklin McCain, Joseph McNeil, David Richmond, Claudette Colvin, and Ruby Bridges?"

"Yes!" Nina and Miles said in unison.

Their mother looked at them with a slight smirk on her face.

"Mama, you have to believe us. We are not making this up!" Nina replied.

"Ma, listen. We also talked with Grandma Lillie's friend Mrs. Emma. You know the lady you call Aunt Cat. She was the one who was on the bus with us and Claudette Colvin. She took us to her house, and we ate sandwiches and tea cookies," Miles explained.

The more Nina and Miles tried to convince their mother that they had indeed been on a journey back in time, the more she found ways to prove them wrong.

"Look, Miles, see on your laptop the last search you did was on the Greensboro four, and, Nina, look at the book you were lying on. There is a picture of Claudette Colvin. Now the whole Ruby Bridges idea, let's you all probably remember me talking about her story a few months ago, when I came back from the conference at Fayetteville State. Now that is enough of all of this nonsense about going back in time and seeing these people."

"See, Nina, I told Grandma Lillie, Ma was not going to believe us," Miles stated in a defeated voice.

"Miles, tell her what Grandma Lillie said," Nina repeated.

"No, you tell her. I am not about to get grounded for a week," Miles replied.

"Why are you two having this conversation as if I am not in the room?" their mother asked

"Mama, can we tell you this one thing without getting in trouble? If you don't believe us after this, we both promise that we will never mention this journey again!" Nina stated.

Miles shook his head in agreement with his sister.

"Alright, Nina. Tell me this last thing, and after this no more of these shenanigans!" their mother stated in a firm voice.

Nina took a deep breath before she shared with her mother the message from Grandma Lillie: "Hmmm, ok. Grandma Lillie told us to tell you that she loved you and she is proud of the woman you have become, Moochie."

The shock on their mother's face was as if she had seen a ghost.

"Ma, are you ok? Maybe you need to sit down," Miles insisted as he rolled his computer chair up to his mother.

Their mother sat there for what felt like hours with her eyes closed, not saying a word. When she finally opened her eyes, tears began to flow down her cheeks. It was clear that their mother realized that Nina and Miles had definitely been on a journey and crossed paths with her beloved grandmother, the only person who ever called her Moochie.

Now the question, is this end or just the beginning of the Historical Adventures of Miles and Nina? Only time will tell, stay tune!

Latasha L. Bethea, MACE, MSW, LCSW is a native of Sanford, NC. She has been ministering through plays, skits, and community events since 2006. She is a graduate of Fayetteville State University, Virginia Commonwealth University, and Union Presbyterian Seminary. She enjoys writing and hosting events that focus on empowering, educating, and equipping people of all ages and backgrounds for Kingdom Living. This is Latasha's first book! Connect with Latasha on Facebook @ DaVine Connections, LLC or Tashab3479@gmail.com

Made in the USA
Middletown, DE
09 May 2022

65549293R00040